T0039883

SELF CARE

Meditations & Inspirations

Self-care has become a new priority—the revelation that it's perfectly permissible to listen to your body and do what it needs.

—FRANCES RYAN

Every act of self-care is a powerful declaration: I am on my side; I am on my side; each day I am more and more on my own side.

—SUSAN WEISS BERRY

Learning to treat ourselves lovingly may at first feel like a dangerous experiment.

—SHARON SALZBERG

It's not selfish to
love yourself, take
care of yourself,
and make your
happiness a priority.
It's necessary.

—MANDY HALE

Take responsibility of your own happiness, never put it in other people's hands.

—ROY T. BENNETT

Choose, every day,
to forgive yourself.
You are human, flawed,
and most of all worthy
of love.

— ALISON MALEE

Of all the judgments we pass in life, none is more important than the judgment we pass on ourselves.

—NATHANIEL BRANDEN

The greatest weapon against stress is our ability to choose one thought over another.

—WILLIAM JAMES

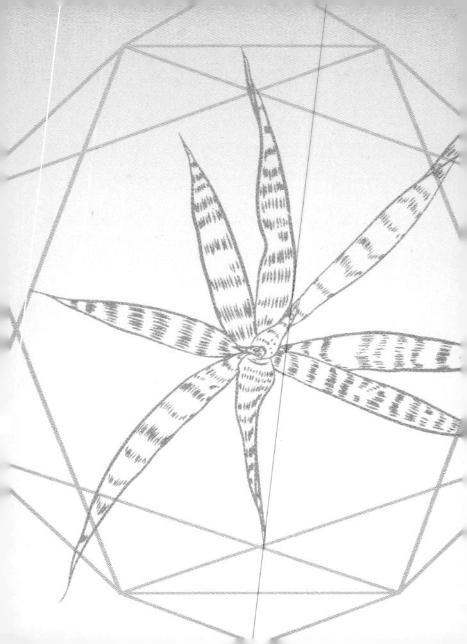

We are what
our thoughts have
made us; so take care
about what you think.
Words are secondary.
Thoughts live; they
travel far.

—SWAMI VIVEKANADA

Beyond a wholesome discipline, be gentle with yourself.

—MAX ERHMANN

If your compassion does not include yourself, it is incomplete.

—JACK KORNFIELD

Forgive yourself.
The supreme act of
forgiveness is when
you can forgive
yourself for all the
wounds you've created
in your own life.

—MIGUEL ANGEL RUIZ

You are imperfect, permanently and inevitably flawed. And you are beautiful.

—AMY BLOOM

And now that
you don't have to
be perfect, you
can be good.

—JOHN STEINBECK

It's always a good idea to do something relaxing prior to making an important decision in your life.

—PAULO COELHO

Fall in love with
yourself until you
finally feel like home.

— JUANSEN DIZON

Low self-esteem is
like driving through
life with your
hand-brake on.

—MAXWELL MALTZ

The best way to cheer yourself is to try to cheer someone else up.

—MARK TWAIN

We have a bad habit, encouraged by pedants and sophisticates, of considering happiness as something rather stupid.

—URSULA K. LE GUIN

It's better to look at the sky than live there.

—TRUMAN CAPOTE

The happiness of your life depends upon the quality of your thoughts.

—MARCUS AURELIUS

There are days
I drop words of
comfort on myself
like falling leaves and
remember that it is
enough to be taken
care of by myself.

—BRIAN ANDREAS

You can't wait
for inspiration.
You have to go
after it with a club.

—JACK LONDON

Too many of us
are not living our
dreams because we
are living our fears.

—LES BROWN

I believe in kindness. Also in mischief. Also in singing, especially when singing is not necessarily prescribed.

—MARY OLIVER

We should consider every day lost on which we have not danced at least once.

—FRIEDRICH NIETZSCHE

If this life is a shipwreck, we must not forget to sing in the lifeboats.

—PETER GAY

Do anything, but let it produce joy.

—WALT WHITMAN

Happiness, to be dissolved into something complete and great.

—WILLA CATHER

Thousands of candles can be lighted from a single candle, and the life of the candle will not be shortened.

Happiness never decreases by being shared.

—THE SOCIETY FOR THE PROMOTION OF BUDDHISM

It is better to light the candle than to curse the darkness.

—WILLIAM L. WATKINSON

We may encounter
many defeats,
but we must not
be defeated.

—MAYA ANGELOU

Don't wait for
other people
to be happy
for you.

Any happiness
you get, you've
got to make
yourself.

—ALICE WALKER

Learn to value yourself, which means: fight for your happiness.

—AYN RAND

To invent your own life's meaning is not easy, but it's still allowed, and I think you'll be happier for the trouble.

—BILL WATTERSON

Can you remember
who you were before
the world told you
who you should be?

—DANIELLE LAPORTE

To be nobody but
yourself in a world
which is doing its best,
night and day, to make
you everybody else

means to fight the
hardest battle which
any human being
can fight; and never
stop fighting.

—e. e. cummings

Taking into account
the public's regrettable
lack of taste, it is
incumbent upon you
not to fit in.

—JANEANE GAROFALO

You're always with yourself, so you might as well enjoy the company.

—DIANE VON FÜRSTENBERG

The mystery of life isn't a problem to solve, but a reality to experience.

—FRANK HERBERT

The art of being happy lies in the power of extracting happiness from common things.

—HENRY WARD BEECHER

Mankind is safer when men seek pleasure than when they seek the power and the glory.

—GEOFFREY GOBER

Give me the luxuries of life and I will willingly do without the necessities.

—FRANK LLOYD WRIGHT

Happiness is where we find it, but very rarely where we seek it.

—JOHN PETIT SENN

The foolish man
seeks happiness
in the distance,
the wise grows it
under his feet.

—JAMES OPPENHEIM

Happiness is not
something you
postpone for the future;
it is something you
design for the present.

—JIM ROHN

It is a strength
to laugh and to
abandon oneself,
to be light.

—FRIDA KAHLO

When I loved
myself enough,
I began leaving
whatever wasn't
healthy. This meant
people, jobs,

my own beliefs
and habits—anything
that kept me small.
My judgment called it
disloyal. Now I see it
as self-loving.

—KIM MCMILLLEN

If we can't laugh
at ourselves, and
at one another,
in good spirit and
without malice,
then what fun
can be left?

—GEORGE TAKEI

I stopped looking for someone to love me. I became that person instead.

—RUDY FRANCISCO

You are not defined by the number of people who like you.

—SADE ANDRIA ZABALA

Don't get high off praises, and don't get too low on critiques.

—JANELLE MONAE

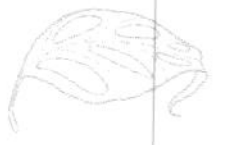

If you look for perfection, you'll never be content.

—LEO TOLSTOY

Life is to be enjoyed, not simply endured. Pleasure and goodness and joy support the pursuit of survival.

—WILLARD GAYLIN

Instead of trying to make your life perfect, give yourself the freedom to make it an adventure, and go ever upward.

—DREW HOUSTON

Each day was
a challenge of
enjoyment, and he
would plan it out as
a field general plans a
campaign.

—A.E. HOTCHNER

A bookworm in bed with a new novel and a good reading lamp is as much prepared for pleasure as a pretty girl at a college dance.

—PHYLLIS MCGINLEY

Happiness is not in the mere possession of money; it lies in the joy of achievement, in the thrill of creative effort.

—FRANKLIN D. ROOSEVELT

I'd far rather
be happy than
right any day.

—DOUGLAS ADAMS

You never
regret being
kind.

—NICOLE SHEPHERD

Pleasure is the object, the duty, and the goal of all rational creatures.

—VOLTAIRE

No need to hurry. No need to sparkle. No need to be anybody but oneself.

—VIRGINIA WOOLF

There is no stress in the world, only people thinking stressful thoughts and then acting on them.

—WAYNE DYER

Your life is already artful—waiting, just waiting, for you to make it art.

—TONI MORRISON

If you cannot be a poet, be the poem.

—DAVID CARRADINE

I am my own
experiment.
I am my own
work of art.

—MADONNA

The secret
to happiness is
freedom . . . and the
secret to freedom
is courage.

—THUCYDIDES

Nothing is better
for self-esteem
than survival.

—MARTHA GELLHORN

Caring for your body,
mind, and spirit is
your greatest and
grandest responsibility.
It's about listening
to the needs of
your soul and then
honoring them.

—KRISTI LING

One of the best ways you can fight discrimination is by taking good care of yourself. Your survival is not just important; it's an act of revolution.

—DASHANNE STOKES

Don't let people pull you into their storm. Pull them into your peace.

—PEMA CHÖDRÖN

This is the real secret of life—to be completely engaged with what you are doing in the here and now.

—ALAN WATTS

You don't have
to see the whole
staircase, just take
the first step.

—MARTIN LUTHER KING, JR.

The mind is its own place, and in itself can make a heaven of hell, a hell of heaven.

—JOHN MILTON

There is a blessed madness in the human need to go against the grain of cold and scarcity.

—MARGARET STARKEY

You see things, and you say, "Why?" But I dream things that never were, and I say, "Why not?"

—GEORGE BERNARD SHAW

No pessimist
ever discovered
the secret of the
stars or sailed an
uncharted land
or opened a new
doorway for the
human spirit.

—HELEN KELLER

Prepare for
mirth, for mirth
becomes a feast.

—WILLIAM SHAKESPEARE

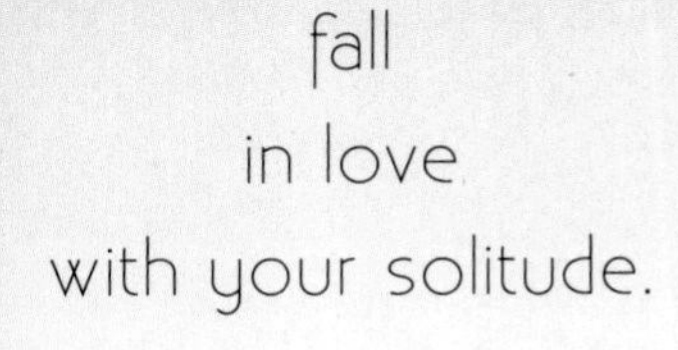

fall
in love
with your solitude.

—RUPI KAUR

How simple and frugal a thing is happiness: a glass of wine, a roast chestnut, a wretched little brazier, the sound of the sea.

Nothing else.

—NIKOS KAZANTZAKIS

Sometimes the most important thing in a whole day is the rest we take between two deep breaths.

—ETTY HILLESUM

Too many people
overvalue what
they are not
and undervalue
what they are.

—MALCOLM S. FORBES

If more of us valued food and cheer and song above hoarded gold, it would be a merrier world.

— J.R.R. TOLKIEN

Too many people spend money they haven't earned to buy things they don't want to impress people they don't like.

—WILL ROGERS

Don't compare yourself to others. You have no idea what their journey is all about.

—REGINA BRETT

Being a successful person is not necessarily defined by what you have achieved, but by what you have overcome.

—FANNIE FLAGG

Don't compare your beginnings to someone else's middle.

—TIM HILLER

Comparison with myself brings improvement, comparison with others brings discontent.

—BETTY JAMIE CHUNG

Accepting yourself
is about respecting
yourself. It's about
honoring yourself
right now, here today,
in this moment.

Not just who you could become somewhere down the line.

—KRIS CARR

Accept who you are. Unless you're a serial killer.

—ELLEN DEGENERES

Time you enjoy wasting is not wasted time.

—MARTHE TROLY-CURTIN

Carve out and claim
time to care for
yourself and kindle
your own fire.

—AMY IPPOLITI

Invent your world.
Surround yourself
with people, color,
sounds, and work
that nourish you.

—SARK

Would you prefer the
happiness of scratching
a mosquito bite or
the happiness of not
having a mosquito bite
in the first place?

—SOGYAL RINPOCHE

I must learn to
be content with
being happier
than I deserve.

—JANE AUSTEN

It's good to do uncomfortable things. It's weight training for life.

—ANNE LAMOTT

For every minute you are angry you lose sixty seconds of happiness.

—RALPH WALDO EMERSON

Human beings make life so interesting. Do you know, that in a universe so full of wonders, they have managed to invent boredom.

—TERRY PRATCHETT

The happiest person is the person who thinks the most interesting thoughts, and we grow happier as we grow older.

—WILLIAM PHELPS

Should a person
do good, let him do
it again and again.
Let him find pleasure
therein, for blissful
is the accumulation
of good.

—THE BUDDHA

Excess on occasion is exhilarating. It prevents moderation from acquiring the deadening effect of a habit.

—W. SOMERSET MAUGHAM

Take time off . . .

The world will
not fall apart
without you.

—MALEBO SEPHODI

Everything in
moderation—
including moderation.

—OSCAR WILDE

Today do
something for you:
Relax, clear your
mind, take a break,
go for a jog, watch
the sunset.

—BROOKE GRIFFIN

When you recover or discover something that nourishes your soul and brings joy, care enough about yourself to make room for it in your life.

—JEAN SHINODA BOLEN

Caring for myself is
not self-indulgence,
it is self-preservation,
and that is an act of
political warfare.

—AUDRE LORDE

I think best in a
hot bath, with my
head tilted back
and my feet up high.

—ELIZABETH JANE HOWARD

Self-care should include the cold shower as well as the scented tub.

—MARY CATHERINE BATESON

Self-care is how you take your power back.

—LALAH DELIA

It is hard to fail, but it is worse never to have tried to succeed.

—THEODORE ROOSEVELT

You can't dump
one cup of sugar
into the ocean and
expect to get syrup. If
everybody sweetened
her own cup of water,
then things would
begin to change.

—FLORYNCE KENNEDY

Life is a series of natural and spontaneous changes. Don't resist them; that only creates sorrow.

Let reality be reality. Let things flow naturally forward in whatever way they like.

—LAOZI

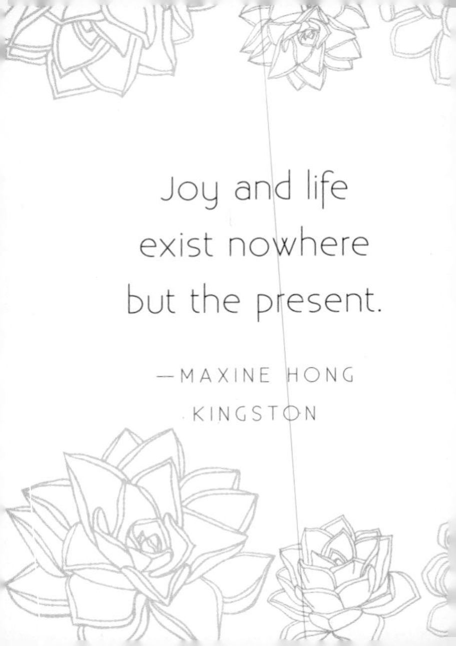

Joy and life
exist nowhere
but the present.

—MAXINE HONG
KINGSTON

The only thing that
will make you happy
is being happy with
who you are, and
not who people
think you are.

—GOLDIE HAWN

Life is always richer
when we're not
playing who we are,
but being who we are.

—BEN KINGSLEY

Be a pineapple:
Stand tall, wear
a crown, and be
sweet on the inside.

—KAT GASKIN

There is only
one corner of
the universe you
can be certain of
improving, and that's
your own self.

—ALDOUS HUXLEY

The road to
success is always
under construction.

—LILY TOMLIN

I would
rather be happy
than dignified.

—CHARLOTTE BRONTË

Stop searching for happiness in the same place you lost it. Change is not dismantling the old, it's building the new.

—BRIANNA WIEST

I love my rejection slips. They show me I tried.

—SYLVIA PLATH

Self-love
seems so often
unrequited.

—ANTHONY POWELL

The most powerful relationship you will ever have is the relationship with yourself.

—STEVE MARABOLI

Live with intention. Walk to the edge. Listen hard. Practice wellness. Play with abandon. Laugh.

Choose with no regret. Do what you love. Live as if this is all there is.

—MARY ANNE RADMACHER

The reason people find it so hard to be happy is that they always see the past better than it was, the present worse than it is, and the future less resolved than it will be.

— MARCEL PAGNOL

Your mind will answer most questions if you learn to relax and wait for the answer.

—WILLIAM S. BURROUGHS

Twenty years from now you will be more disappointed by the things that you didn't do than by the ones you did do.

So throw off the bowlines. Sail away from the safe harbor. Catch the trade winds in your sails. Explore. Dream. Discover.

—MARK TWAIN

Of all forms of caution, caution in love is perhaps the most fatal to true happiness.

—BERTRAND RUSSELL

Life is a combination of magic and pasta.

—FEDERICO FELLINI

Nourishing yourself in a way that helps you blossom in the direction you want to go is attainable, and you are worth the effort.

—DEBORAH DAY

It is not abstinence from pleasures that is best, but mastery over them without being worsted.

—ARISTIPPUS

When admiring other people's gardens, don't forget to tend to your own flowers.

—SANOBER KHAN

Happiness is a choice that requires effort at times.

—AESCHYLUS

When you accept
you have to rescue
yourself, then
you're adulting.

—SHARON PEARSON

Self-care is giving the world the best of you, instead of what's left of you.

—KATIE REED

Self-care is not selfish. You cannot serve from an empty vessel.

—ELEANOR BROWNN

Have patience with all things, but first with yourself.

—ST. FRANCIS DE SALES

No one serves
their friends by
grinding themselves
into dust on the
altar of compassion.

—SEANAN MCGUIRE

Don't work so
hard that you forget
to enjoy your life.

—AKIROQ BROST

You aren't doing "nothing" when you choose to put your well-being first. In fact, this is the key to having everything.

—BRITTANY BURGUNDER

Don't ask what the world needs. Ask what makes you come alive and go do it. Because what the world needs are more people who have come alive.

—HOWARD THURMAN

When you can't
find your purpose
in a day, make
it to look after
yourself.

—DODIE CLARK

Observe your comfort level when it comes to being good to yourself. Discomfort is a wise teacher.

—CAROLINE MYSS

Life shrinks
or expands in
proportion to
one's courage.

—ANAÏS NIN

The most terrifying thing is to accept oneself completely.

—CARL JUNG

Letting go is
an inside job,
something only we
can do for ourselves.

—SHARON SALZBERG

We are strong enough to stand tall tearlessly, we are brave enough to bend to cry, and we are sad enough to know that we must laugh again.

—NIKKI GIOVANNI

No more
martyring myself.

—SHARON E. RAINEY

After joy, grief;
after grief, joy.

—TAMIL PROVERB

Take rest; a field
that has rested gives
a bountiful crop.

—OVID

Talk to yourself like you would to someone you love.

—BRENÉ BROWN

Take care of your body. It's the only place you have to live.

—JIM ROHN

When the body forces you to stop, it's saying, "Hey buddy, you've gone too far."

—JACQUELINE ESCOLME

Setting boundaries
is a way of caring
for myself. It doesn't
make me mean,
selfish, or uncaring
because I don't do
things your way. I care
about me too.

—CHRISTINE MORGAN

Take care of your mind, your body will thank you. Take care of your body, your mind will thank you.

—DEBBIE HAMPTON

Though no one can
go back and make
a brand-new start,
anyone can start
from now and make
a brand-new ending.

—CARL BARD

When we self-regulate well, we are better able to control the trajectory of our emotional lives and resulting actions based on our values and sense of purpose.

—AMY LEIGH MERCREE

Replace your
vicious stress cycle
with a vicious cycle
of self-care.

—DR. SARA GOTTFRIED

Our soul is like a soft and gentle flower, it needs to be nurtured, cared for, tended to, with sufficient sunlight,

fresh air, and freedom
to bloom into its
most precious and
beautiful form. This,
my friend, is self-love.

—MIYA YAMANOUCHI

If we give our children sound self-love, they will be able to deal with whatever life puts before them.

— bell hooks

One does not
get better, but
different and older,
and that is always
a pleasure.

—GERTRUDE STEIN

We can't be so
desperate for love
that we forget
where we can
always find it:
within.

—ALEXANDRA ELLE

Everybody is different, and every body is different.

—BEVERLY DIEHL

Do something every day that is loving toward your body and gives you the opportunity to enjoy the sensations of your body.

—GOLDA PORETSKY

The love and attention you always thought you wanted from someone else is the love and attention you first need to give to yourself.

—BRYANT MCGILLNS

Your time is way too valuable to be wasting on people that can't accept who you are.

—TURCOIS OMINEK

Don't waste your energy trying to change opinions. Do your thing, and don't care if they like it.

—TINA FEY

It's all about falling in love with yourself and sharing that love with someone who appreciates you, rather than looking for love to compensate for a self-love deficit.

—EARTHA KITT

Don't be reckless with other people's hearts, don't put up with those who are reckless with yours.

—BAZ LUHRMANN

You've got to learn to leave the table when love's no longer being served.

—NINA SIMONE

If you do not respect your own wishes, no one else will. You will simply attract people who disrespect you as much as you do.

—VIRONIKA TUGALEVA

When you take care of yourself, you're a better person for others. When you feel good about yourself, you treat others better.

—SOLANGE KNOWLES

Self-care is taking all the pressures you are facing right now, and deciding to which you will respond, and how.

—IMANI SHOLA

Most people
are about as
happy as they
make up their
minds to be.

—ABRAHAM LINCOLN

They called her witch because she knew how to heal herself.

—TÉ V. SMITH

You may be the only person left who believes in you, but it's enough. It takes just one star to pierce a universe of darkness. Never give up.

—RICHELLE E. GOODRICH

You have been criticizing yourself for years, and it hasn't worked. Try approving of yourself and see what happens.

—LOUISE L. HAY

Self-discipline
is self-caring.

—M. SCOTT PECK

People pleasing doesn't allow you to receive.

—ABIOLA ABRAMS

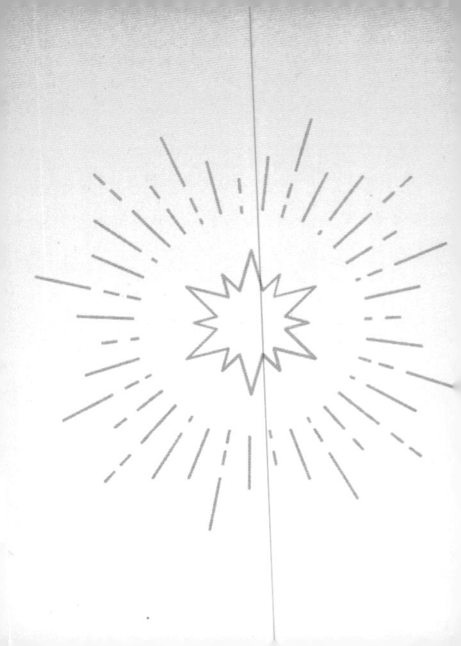

You can't take care of anyone else unless you first take care of yourself.

—MICHAEL HYATT

The fact that someone else loves you doesn't rescue you from the project of loving yourself.

—SAHAJ KOHLI

Love yourself enough to set boundaries. Your time and energy are precious. You get to choose how you use it.

—ANNA TAYLOR

The only person you shouldn't be able to live without is you.

—CHRIS MCGEOWN

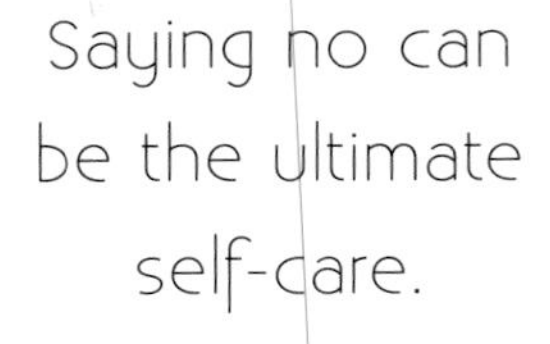

Saying no can be the ultimate self-care.

—CLAUDIA BLACK

Self-care is never selfish, but it may feel that way when you live a frenzied life.

—ARTHUR P. CIARAMICOLI

For those of you who
struggle with guilt
regarding self-care,
answer this question:
What greater gift can
you give to those
you love than your
own wholeness?

—SHANNON TANNER

When I went to school, they asked me what I wanted to be when I grew up. I wrote down "Happy."

They told me I didn't understand the assignment, and I told them they didn't understand life.

—JOHN LENNON

Caring for your
body, mind, and
spirit is your greatest
and grandest
responsibility. It's
about listening to
the needs of your
soul and then
honoring them.

—KRISTI LING

I have an everyday religion that works for me. Love yourself first, and everything else falls into line.

—LUCILLE BALL

Be patient with yourself. Self-growth is tender; it's holy ground. There's no greater investment.

—STEPHEN COVEY

Acknowledge,
accept, and honor
that you deserve
your own deepest
compassion and love.

—NANETTE MATHEWS